Prepare Word Family Spelling

Word FAMILY

M.A. in English Literature

This book is specially designed for those kids who wants to prepare word family spellings. Regular practice of this book, kids will develop a clear concept of word family and their group words.

Majumdar

-ack

attack
back
black
crack
hack
Jack
knack
lack
pack
quack
rack
sack
snack
stack
tack
track
whack
Zack

-ad

ad
bad
brad
cad
clad
dad
dood
ad
glad
had
lad
mad
pad
sad

-ail

ail
fail
hail
jail
mail
nail
pail
rail
sail
snail
tail
wail

Prepare Word Family Spelling

-ain	-ake	-ale
brain	awake	ale
chain	bake	bale
complain	brake	dale
explain	cake	gale
gain	fake	kale
grain	flake	male
main	Jake	pale
obtain	lake	sale
pain	make	scale
plain	quake	stale
rain	rake	tale
slain	sake	whale
Spain	shake	
sprain	snake	
stain	stake	
strain	take	
train	wake	
vain		

Prepare Word Family Spelling

-all

all
ball
call
fall
gall
hall
install
mall
small
squall
stall
tall
thrall
wall

-am

cam
clam
dam
dram
exam
gram
ham
jam
lam
ma'am
Pam
ram
Sam
scam
slam
spam
swam
tam
tram
wham
yam

-ame

blame
came
fame
flame
frame
game
lame
name
same
shame
tame

-an

an
ban
bran
can
clan
Dan
Fan
flan
Fran
Jan
Japan
man
pan
pecan
plan
ran
scan
span
Stan
tan
than
van

-ank

bank
blank
crank
dank
drank
flank
frank
Hank
plank
prank
rank
sank
shrank
spank
tank
thank
yank

-ap

cap
clap
flap
gap
lap
map
nap
rap
sap
scrap
slap
snap
strap
tap
trap
wrap
yap
zap

Prepare Word Family Spelling

-ar

afar
bar
car
czar
far
gar
guitar
jar
mar
par
scar
spar
star
tar
tsar

-ash

ash
bash
brash
cash
clash
crash
dash
flash
gash
gnash
hash
lash
mash
rash
sash
slash
smash
splash
stash
thrash
trash

-at

at
bat
brat
cat
chat
fat
flat
gnat
hat
mat
pat
rat
sat
slat
spat
tat
that
vat

-ate

abate
ate
crate
date
debate
fate
gate
grate
hate
Kate
late
mate
plate
rate
relate
sate
skate
state

-aw

caw
claw
draw
flaw
gnaw
jaw
law
paw
raw
saw
slaw
straw
thaw

-ay

away
bay
bray
clay
day
decay
delay
display
flay
gray
hay
jay
lay
may
nay
okay
pay
play
pray
quay
ray
relay
replay
say
slay
spray
stay
stray
sway
they
today
tray
way

Prepare Word Family Spelling

-eat

beat
cheat
cleat
eat
feat
greet
heat
meat
neat
peat
pleat
seat
treat
wheat

-eel

eel
feel
heel
keel
kneel
peel
reel
steel
wheel

-eep

beep
creep
deep
jeep
keep
peep
seep
sheep
sleep
steep
sweep
weep

-eet	-ell	-en
beet	bell	amen
feet	cell	Ben
fleet	dell	children
greet	dwell	den
meet	farew	fen
sheet	ell	gentlemen
sleet	fell	glen
street	hell	Gwen
sweet	sell	hen
tweet	shell	men
	smell	open
	spell	pen
	swell	then
	tell	ten
	well	when
	yell	wren
		yen

-ent

accent
bent
cent
dent
event
gent
lent
rent
scent
sent
spent
tent
vent
went

-est

best
chest
crest
jest
nest
pest
quest
rest
test
unrest
vest
west
zest

-ice

dice
ice
mice
nice
price
rice
slice
spice
splice
thrice
twice
vice

-ick	-ide	-ife
brick	bride	fife
chick	decide	knife
click	glide	life
flick	hide	strife
kick	pride	wife
lick	ride	
nick	side	
pick	slide	
quick	stride	
Rick	tide	
sick	wide	
slick		
stick		
thick		
tick		
trick		
wick		

-ight

bright
delight
fight
flight
fright
height
knight
light
might
night
plight
right
sight
slight
tight
tonight

-ile

bile
file
mile
Nile
pile
rile
smile
stile
tile
vile
while

-ill

bill
chill
dill
drill
fill
frill
gill
grill
hill
ill
Jill
kill
krill
mill
pill
quill
shrill
sill
skill
spill
still
swill
thrill
thrill
till
trill
will

-in	-ine	-ing
bin	brine	bring
chin	decline	cling
din	define	fling
fin	dine	king
gin	fine	ping
grin	line	ring
in	mine	sing
kin	nine	sling
pin	pine	spring
shin	shine	sting
skin	shrine	string
sin	sine	swing
spin	spine	thing
thin	swine	wing
tin	tine	wring
twin	twine	zing
win	vine	
within	whine	
	wine	

-ink

blink
brink
drink
fink
ink
link
mink
pink
rink
shrink
sink
stink
think
wink

-ip

blip
chip
dip
drip
flip
grip
hip
lip
nip
quip
rip
ship
sip
skip
slip
snip
strip
tip
trip
whip
zip

-it

admit
bit
fit
flit
grit
hit
it
kit
knit
lit
mit
pit
quit
sit
skit
slit
snit
spit
split
twit
wit

-oat	-ock	-og
boat	block	blog
coat	clock	bog
float	cock	catalog
gloat	crock	clog
goat	dock	cog
oat	flock	dog
stoat	frock	fog
throat	hock	frog
	jock	hog
	knock	jog
	lock	log
	mock	slog
	o’clock	smog
	rock	
	shock	
	smock	
	sock	
	stock	

-oil

boil
broil
coil
foil
oil
soil
spoil
toil

-oke

awoke
bloke
broke
choke
joke
poke
smoke
spoke
stoke
stroke
woke
yoke

-oo

boo
coo
goo
igloo
moo
shoo
too
woo
zoo

Prepare Word Family Spelling

-ood	-oof	-ook
good	goof	book
hood	proof	brook
stood	roof	cook
wood	spoof	crook
brood	hoof	hook
food	woof	look
mood		nook
		rook
		shook
		took

Prepare Word Family Spelling

-oom	-ool	-oon
bloom	cool	balloon
boom	drool	goon
broom	fool	loon
doom	pool	moon
gloom	spool	noon
groom	stool	soon
loom	tool	spoon
room		swoon
zoom		

-oop	-oot	-op
coop	boot	bop
droop	hoot	chop
hoop	scoot	cop
loop	shoot	crop
scoop	foot	drop
snoop	soot	flop
stoop		hop
troop		lop
		mop
		plop
		pop
		prop
		sop
		shop
		stop
		top

-ore

bore
chore
core
fore
gore
lore
more
ore
pore
score
shore
sore
spore
store
swore
tore
wore
yore

-orn

adorn
born
corn
forlorn
horn
morn
scorn
shorn
thorn
torn
worn

-ot

apricot
blot
bot
clot
cot
dot
forgot
got
hot
jot
knot
lot
not
plot
pot
rot
shot
slot
spot
tot
trot

Prepare Word Family Spelling

-ought

bought
brought
fought
ought
sought
thought
wrought

-ould

could
should
would

-ouse

douse
grouse
house
louse
mouse
spouse

-out	-ow	-own
about	bow	brown
bout	cow	crown
clout	chow	down
gout	how	drown
grout	now	frown
out	plow	gown
lout	sow	nightgown
pout	vow	town
scout	wow	
shout	crow	
snout	flow	
spout	glow	
stout	grow	
tout	low	
trout	mow	
	row	
	show	
	slow	
	snow	
	sow	
	stow	
	throw	
	tow	

-uck

buck
chuck
cluck
duck
luck
muck
puck
pluck
stuck
struck
truck
tuck
yuck

-ug

bug
dug
hug
jug
lug
mug
plug
pug
rug
shrug
smug
snug
thug
tug

-ump

bump
clump
dump
grump
hump
jump
lump
plump
pump
rump
slump
stump
thump
trump

-un

bun
fun
gun
nun
pun
run
shun
spun
stun
sun

-unk

bunk
chunk
drunk
dunk
flunk
funk
hunk
junk
lunk
plunk
punk
skunk
slunk
spunk
sunk
trunk

www.ingramcontent.com/pod-product-compliance
Lightning Source LLC
LaVergne TN
LVHW021326160826
845679LV00001B/493